NBA ALL ST

basketball coloring book

THIS BOOK BELONGS TO :

_____

NBA ALL STARS 20 21 20

basketball coloring book

Players List

kawhi leonard	1
James Harden	2
LeBron James	3
Joel Embiid	4
Stephen Curry	5
Kemba Walker	6
Giannis Antetokounmpo	7
Kevin Durant	8
Anthony Davis	9
Russell Westbrook	10
Paul George	11
Klay Thompson	12
Karl-Anthony Towns	13
Blake Griffin	14
Damian Lillard	15
Kevin Love	16
Rudy Gobert	17
Ben Simmons	18
victor oladipo	19
jimmy butler	20
demar derozan	21
Zion WIlliamson	22

JAMES HARDEN

CURRENT TEAM:
HOUSTON ROCKETS

HEIGHT: 1.96 M
WEIGHT: 99.8 KG

STEPHEN CURRY

WEIGHT: 86 KG
HEIGHT: 1.91 M

CURRENT TEAM:

GOLDEN STATE WARRIORS

KEMBA WALKER

HEIGHT: 1.83 M

WEIGHT: 84 KG

CURRENT TEAM:

BOSTON CELTICS

GIANNIS
ANTETOKOUNMPO

HEIGHT: 2.11 M

WEIGHT: 110 KG

CURRENT TEAM:

MILWAUKEE BUCKS

KEVIN DURANT

HEIGHT: 2.08 M

WEIGHT: 109 KG

CURRENT TEAM:

BROOKLYN NETS

RUSSELL
WESTBROOK
HEIGHT: 1.91 M
WEIGHT: 91 KG
CURRENT TEAM:
WASHINGTON WIZARDS

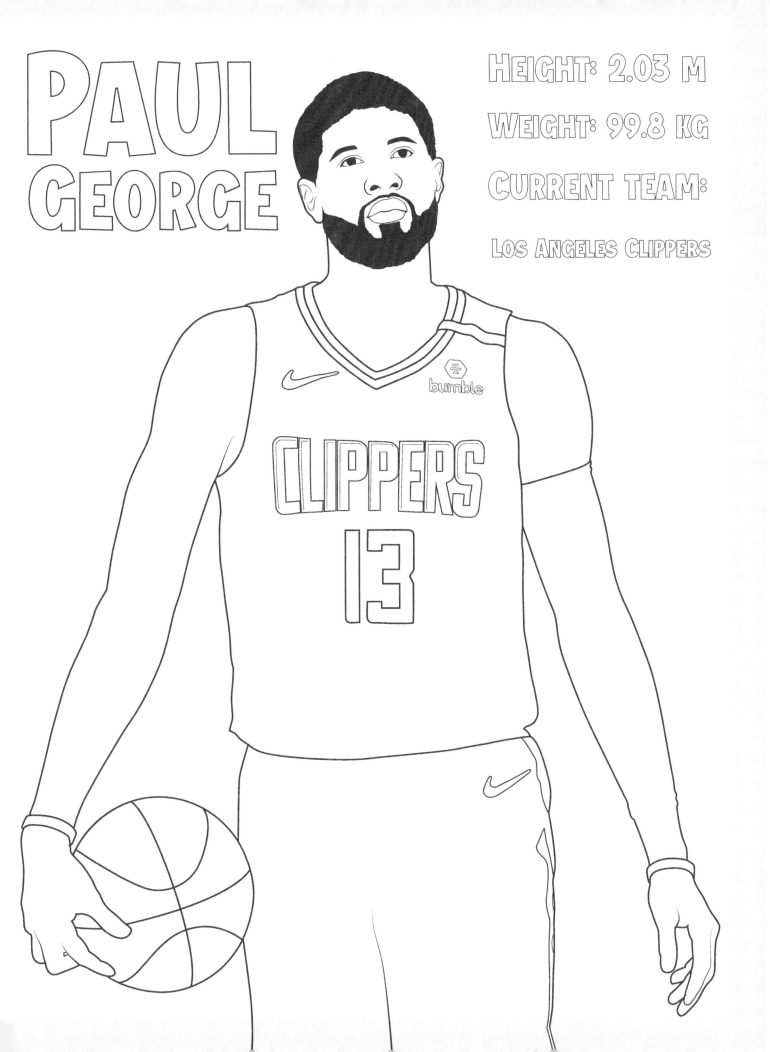

PAUL GEORGE

HEIGHT: 2.03 M
WEIGHT: 99.8 KG
CURRENT TEAM:
LOS ANGELES CLIPPERS

DAMIAN LILLARD

HEIGHT: 1.88 M

WEIGHT: 88 KG

CURRENT TEAM:

PORTLAND TRAIL BLAZERS

BEN
SIMMONS

HEIGHT: 2.08 M
WEIGHT: 109 KG
CURRENT TEAMS:
PHILADELPHIA 76ERS

DEMAR DEROZAN

HEIGHT: 1.98 M

WEIGHT: 99.8 KG

CURRENT TEAM:

SAN ANTONIO SPURS

Made in the USA
Coppell, TX
06 July 2024

34339897R00031